Stuck, Sprayed, and Scrawled: an Ode to Graffiti

By Grant Schrader
(with much thanks to my wife Sabrina Saenz-Schrader)

Index

I. Introduction	pg. 3
1. Puro Viaje	pg. 4
2. Blue	pg. 5
3. One word	pg. 6
4. Clear message	pg. 7
5. Four words, one unicorn	pg. 8
6. 12 Gauge Promise	pg. 9
7. Made you look	pg. 10
8. Electric box	pg. 11
9. Tagged door	pg. 12
10. Trio	pg. 13
11. Chained	pg. 14
12. Crosswalk	pg. 15
13. Short wall by greenscape	pg. 16
14. Buffing, The Vampire Slayer	pg. 17
15. Statement	pg. 18
16. Confusion	pg. 19
17. Memories	pg. 20
18. Familiar	pg. 21
19. Trashcan	pg. 22
20. Green	pg. 23
21. Sign	pg. 24
22. Positive	pg. 25
23. Box	pg. 26
24. ENLUV	pg. 27
25. Countless	pg. 28
26. The 8	pg. 29
27. Fox	pg. 30
28. Blog link and Legal	pg. 31

I.

Introduction

I do not take the materials I've placed between these pages lightly. I understand that graffiti is an egregious event, and yet I see it as art. Consider its storied history; scratching on walls and buildings placed long before those who malign it today were born. With such a legacy, graffiti stands out as a factor of the human mind; striking out with the purpose of rebellion, informing, or the creation of something of beauty in the realm of the mundane. Like a lost continent, the borders surrounding art are indeterminate; in one hand is someone like Robert Rauschenberg painting a white canvas white, and on the other Guillermo Vargas Jimenez, who went as far as starving a dog in pursuit of the incorporeal limits of the definition of "Art". Thus I submit for your consideration these 27 poems. The images depicted were made with ink and words, and by ink and words I mean to exculpate them out of the collective consciousness as a form of crime, and into the realm of art. I hope you enjoy reading and viewing my words and pictures even one bit as much as I have writing and photographing them, then I shall have supplied you with a piece of literature you will enjoy and share for a lifetime.

<u>Puro Viaje</u>

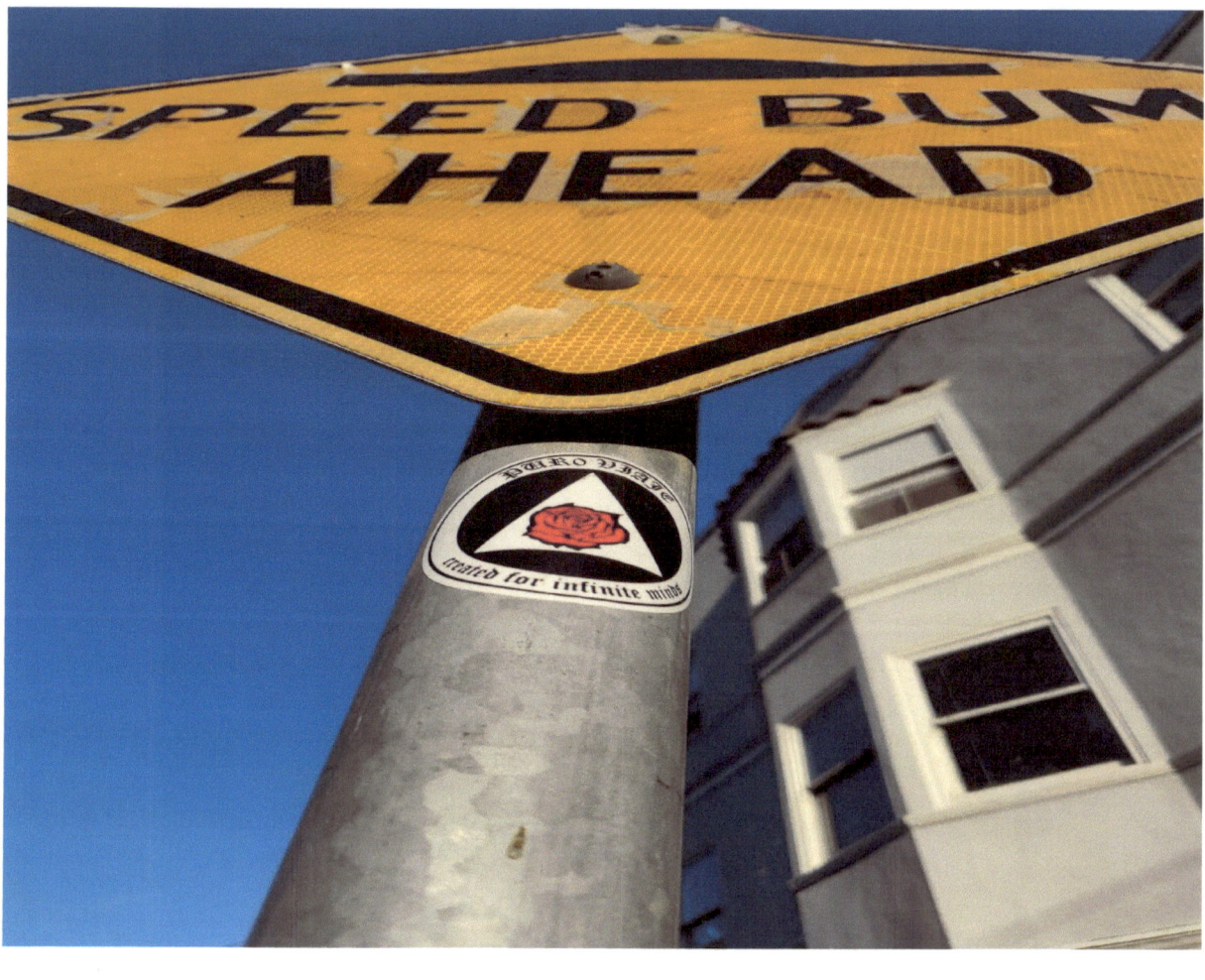

Above: Puro Viaje
Below: Created for infinite minds

These words encircle a black ball
containing a white triangle,
itself home to
a red rose.

Blue

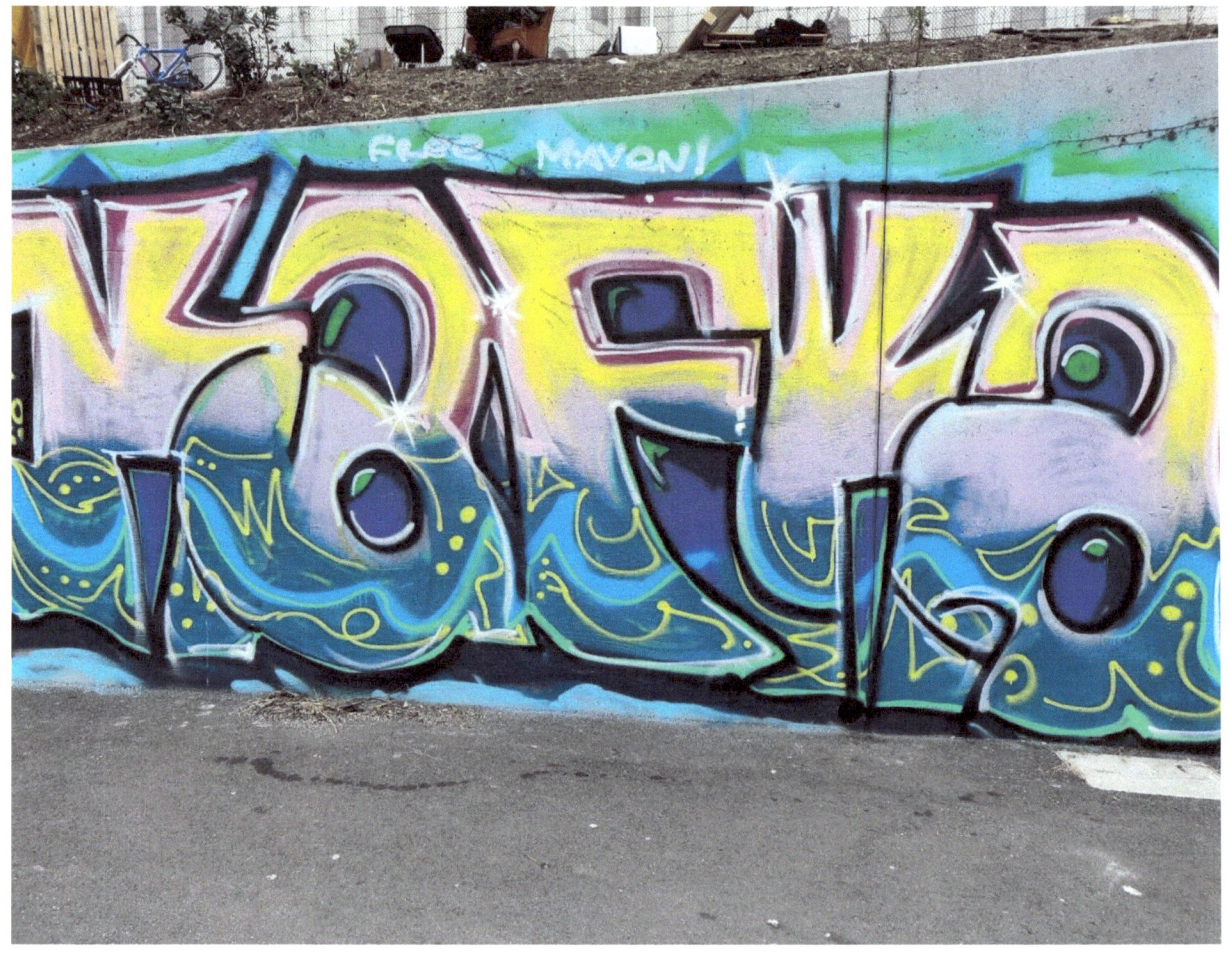

In bright colors,
dandelion yellow,
teal,
light neon blue,
purple,
and sharp letters
reads:
"Kafka".
Above: "Free Maven!"

<u>One Word</u>

Red ink
on Bart
station walls
Cittiezz

<u>Clear Message</u>

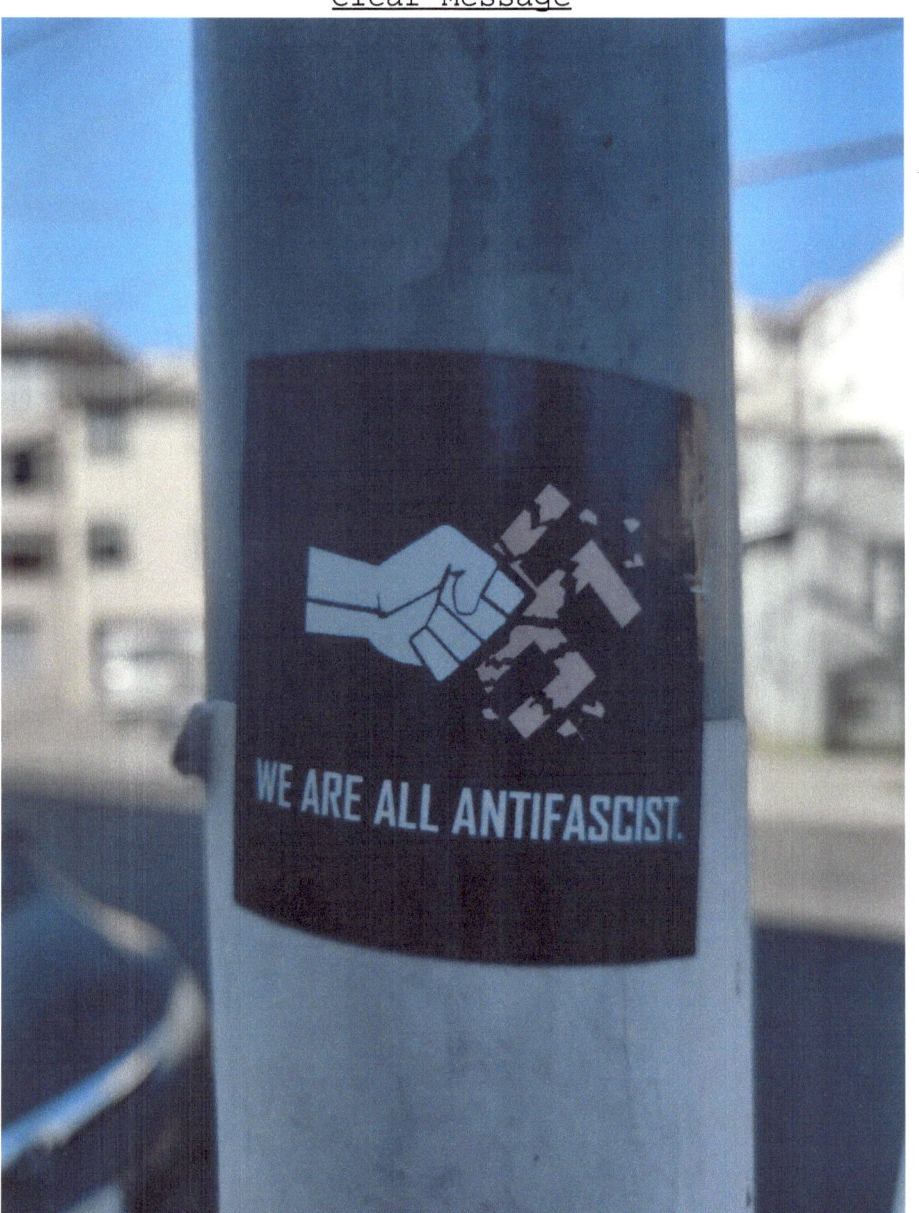

Black square
White fist
fracturing
red swastika
text(in white):
"WE ARE ALL ANTIFASCIST".

<u>Four Words, One Unicorn</u>

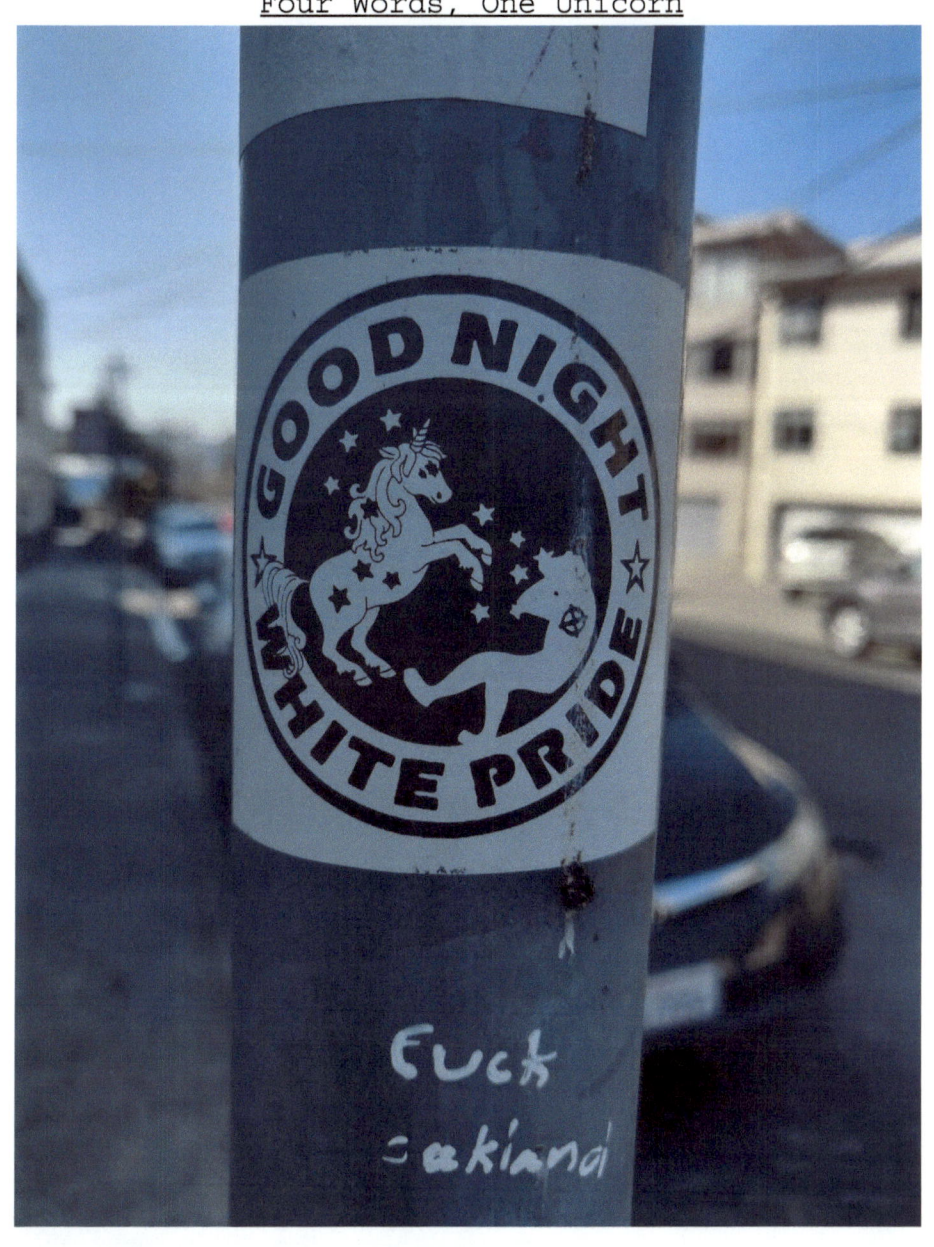

Black rimmed circle
black text on white background reads:
"Good Night"
(then two five pointed stars)
"White Pride."
A white unicorn in a field of black, surrounded by white stars,
rears against a cowering white figure, with a circle and x.

Bonus:
Below,
in white paint- "Fuck Oakland"

<u>12 Gauge Promise</u>

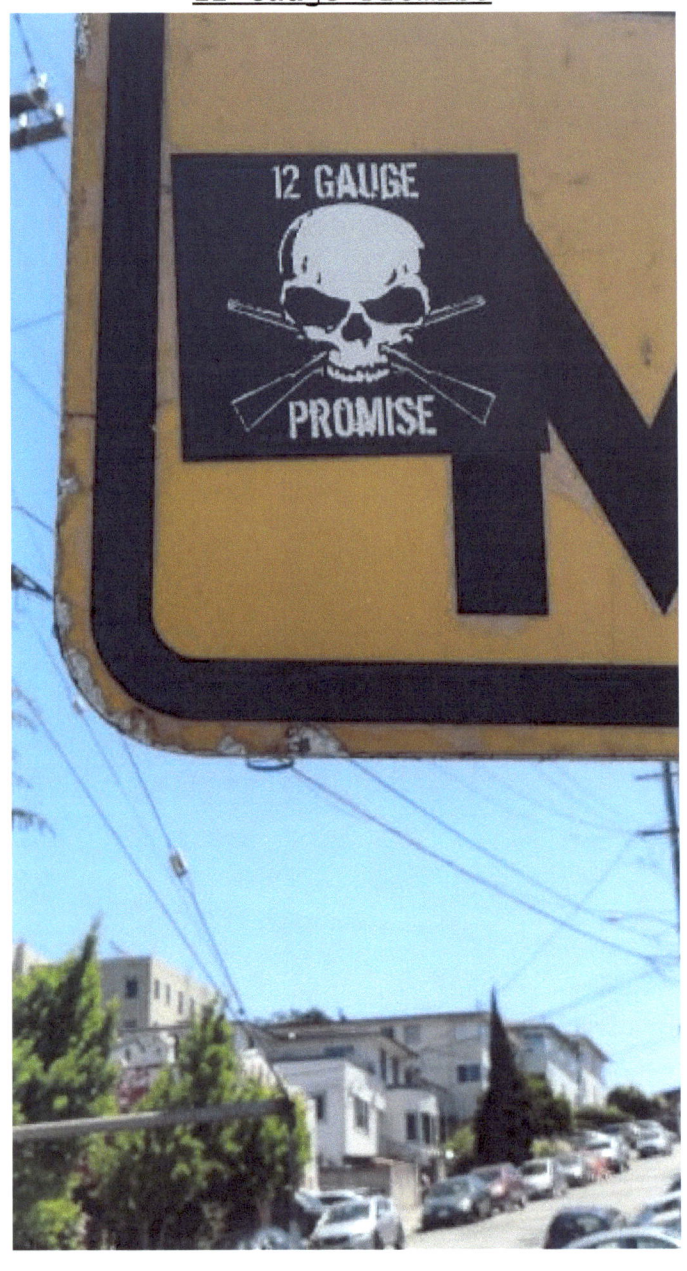

"12 GAUGE"
Skull
with crossed shotguns
behind it
"PROMISE"
underneath.
Suspeded within
a black square.

<u>Made You Look</u>

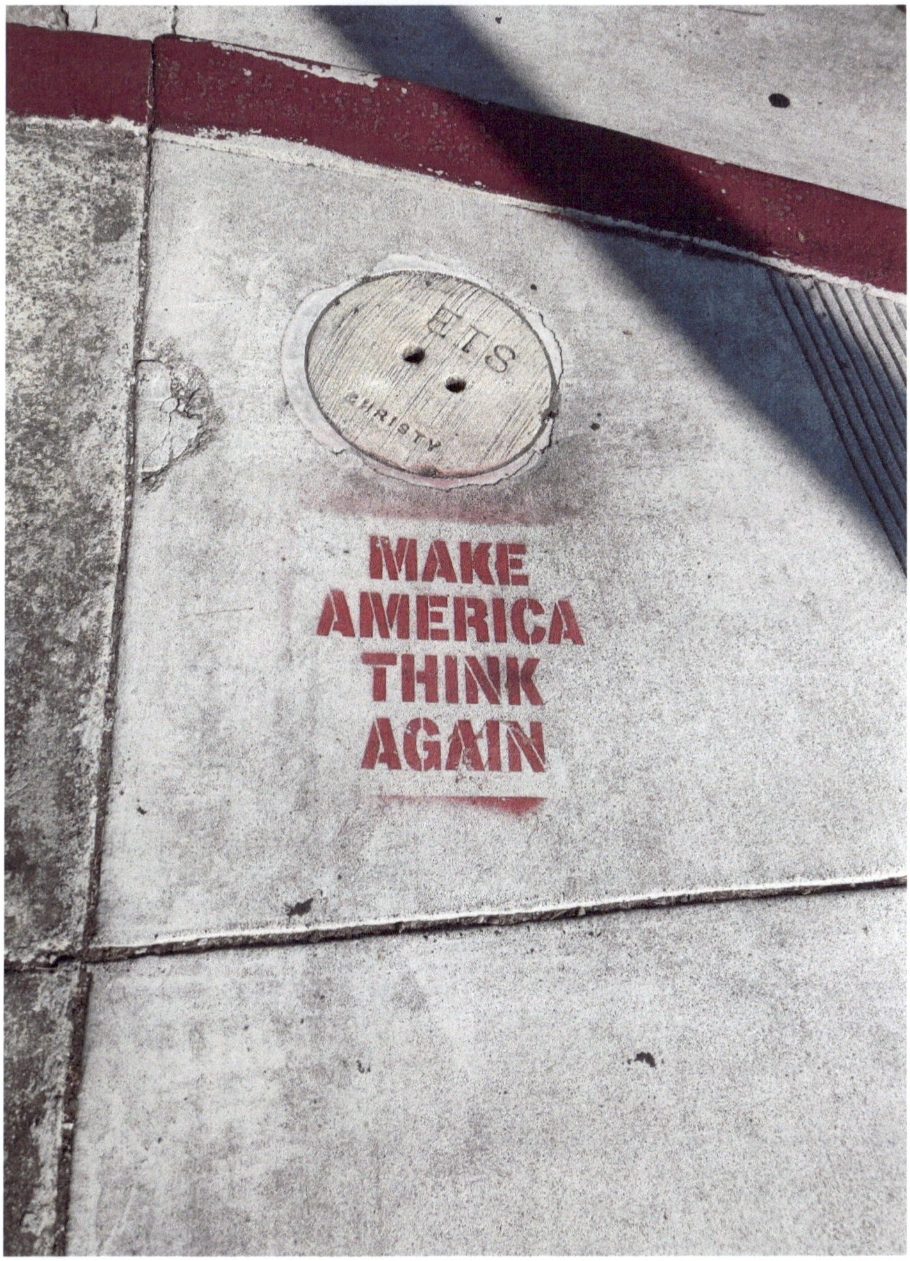

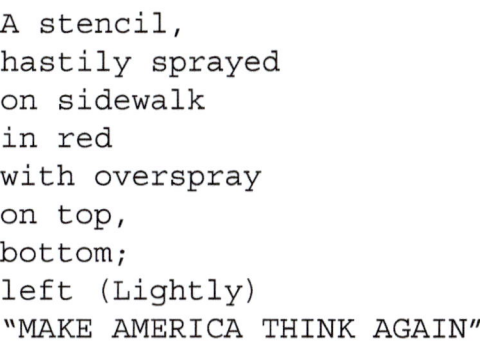

A stencil,
hastily sprayed
on sidewalk
in red
with overspray
on top,
bottom;
left (Lightly)
"MAKE AMERICA THINK AGAIN"

<u>Electric Box</u>

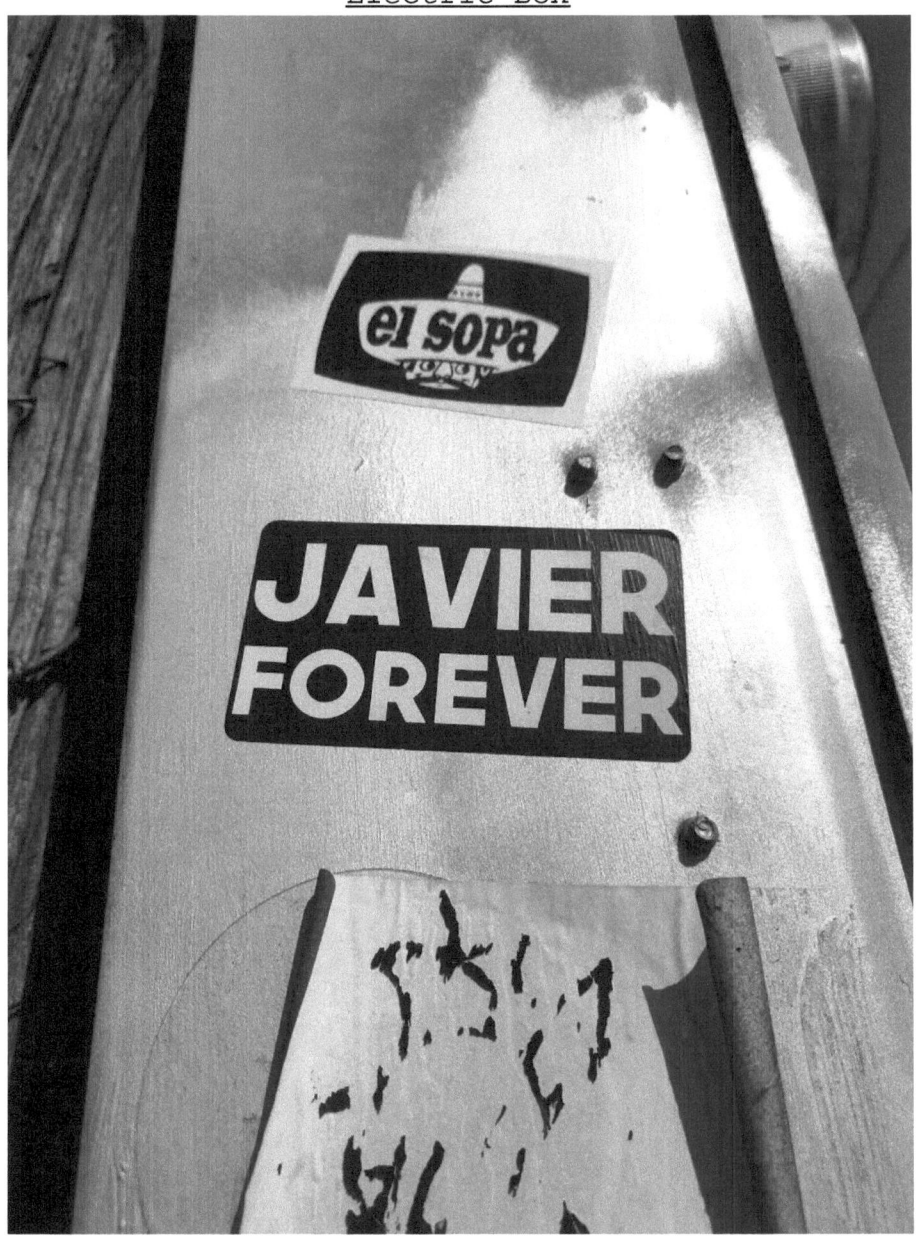

Stuck on an electric box,
oh so high
two stickers,
both black.
The top one
contains a mustachioed man
wearing a sombrero.
The text (in black) on its large rim
reads "el sopa"
The lower states simply (in white text):
"Javier Forever"

<u>Door</u>

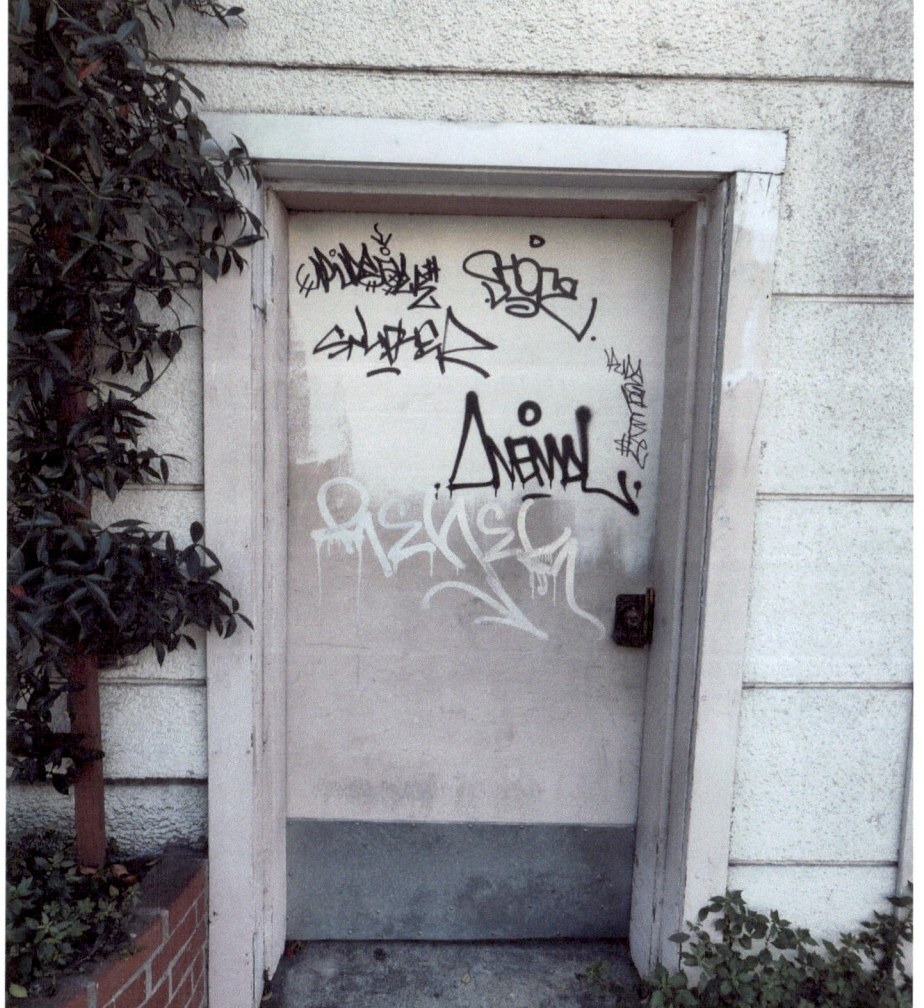

Upon your pinkish white skin
6 recently left their mark.
Some left Script embellished with lines, arrows, and dots.
Another, also in black, could say "snyder", its letters
crammed together.
Another, running vertically,
could be mistaken for a scrawled
script.
Off to the left of center, a
word with a triangular sail;
could be "anemal",
and under that,
one of the acrylic kings
of oakland,
in a shimmering silver
"Renek".

Trio

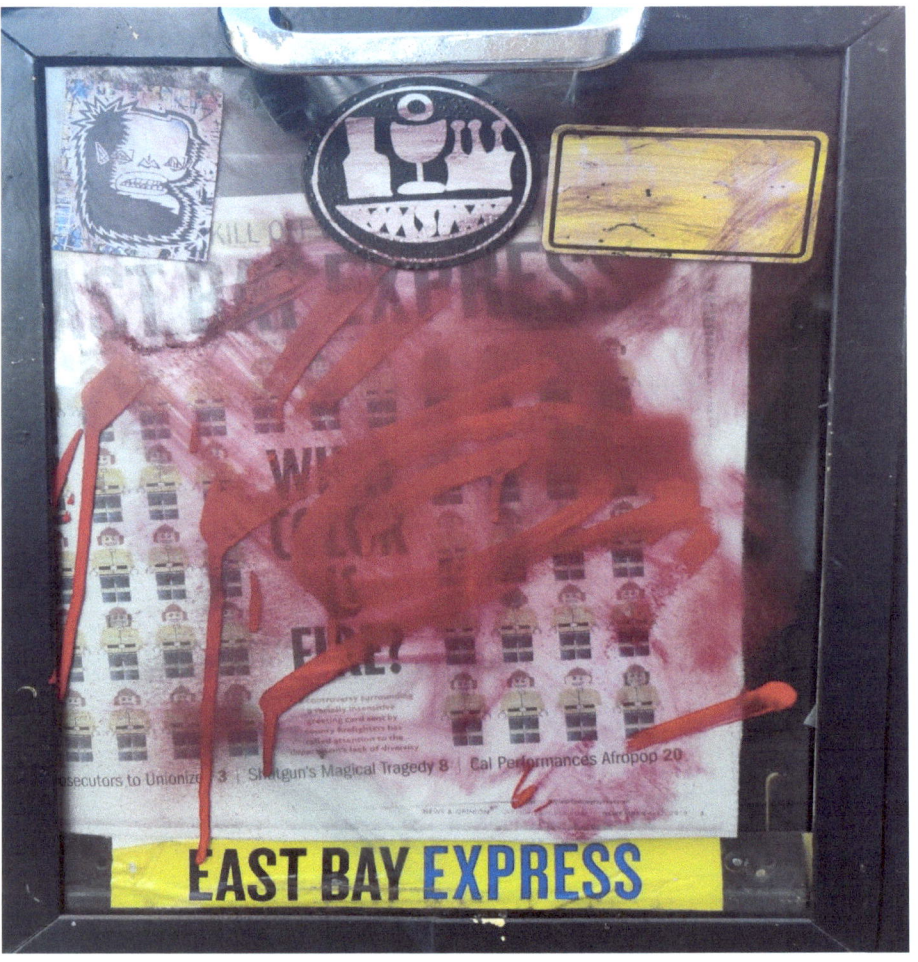

The East Bay Express
left their property in the street
furnishing canvas for three
entrepreneurial artists.
One left a troll, with ragged
beard suspended in a rectangular
plane, beset by strange shapes and colors.
The second placed a round
black sticker displaying
a bottle, a chalice, and crown.
The third remains faded,
only a yellow rectangle,
with a black stripe
skirting its borders.
Another, more abstract stance was made,
as some passer by left a flurry of red paint
on the box's face.

<u>Chained</u>

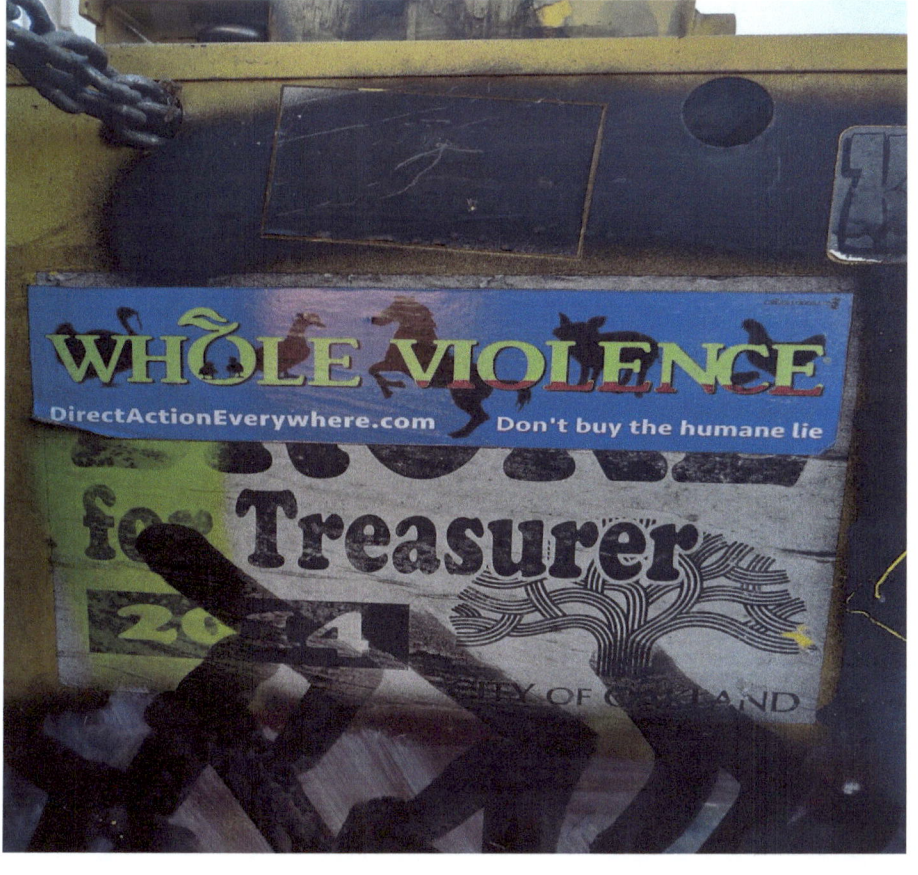

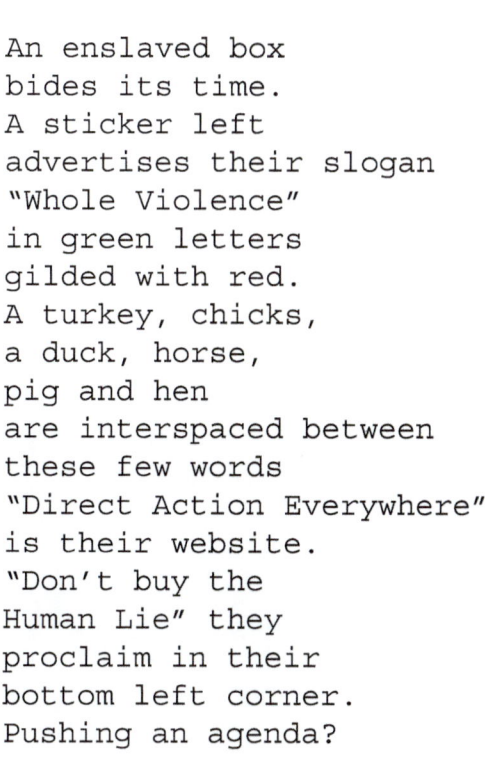

An enslaved box
bides its time.
A sticker left
advertises their slogan
"Whole Violence"
in green letters
gilded with red.
A turkey, chicks,
a duck, horse,
pig and hen
are interspaced between
these few words
"Direct Action Everywhere"
is their website.
"Don't buy the
Human Lie" they
proclaim in their
bottom left corner.
Pushing an agenda?

<u>Crosswalk</u>

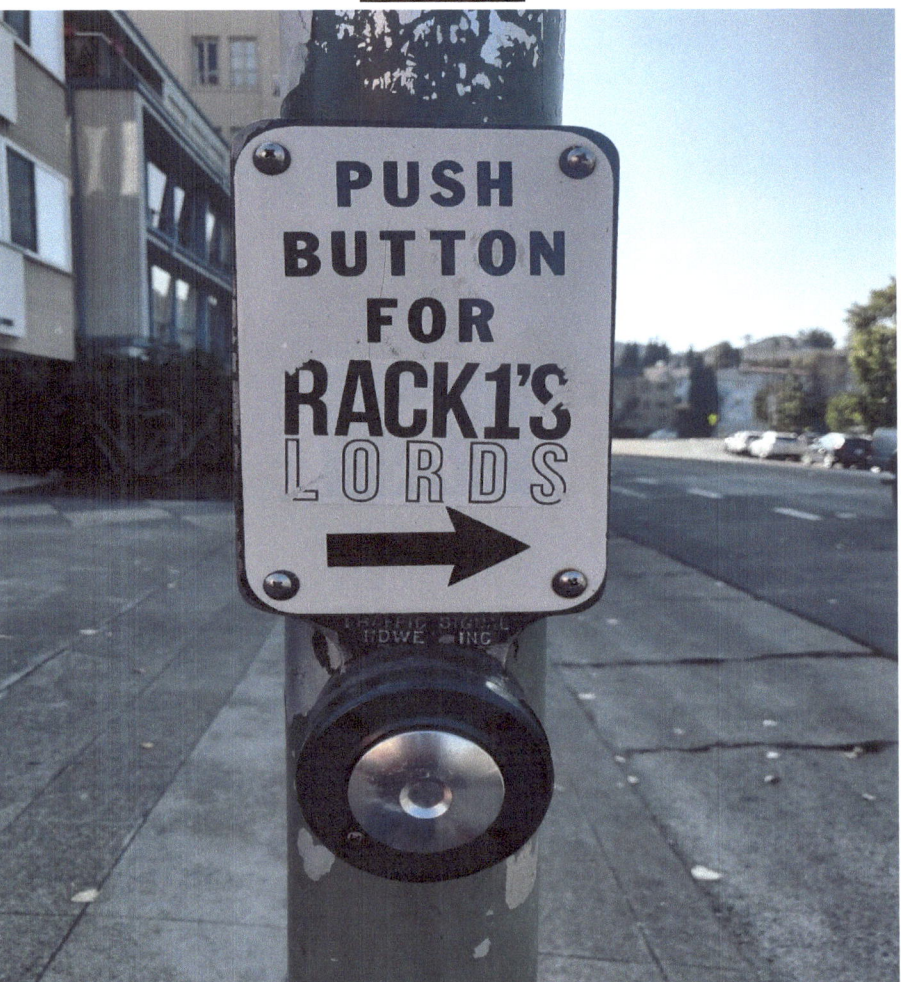

On the pole at the light
a collaboration was made.
The city with their
half of the message,
the graffito with theirs.
Immaculate text reads
"Push button for"
while the remainder
(on a rectangular white sticker)
reads (in black)
"Rack 1's
LORDS"
with the latter word being
white with a black outline.

16

<u>Short Wall by Greenscape</u>

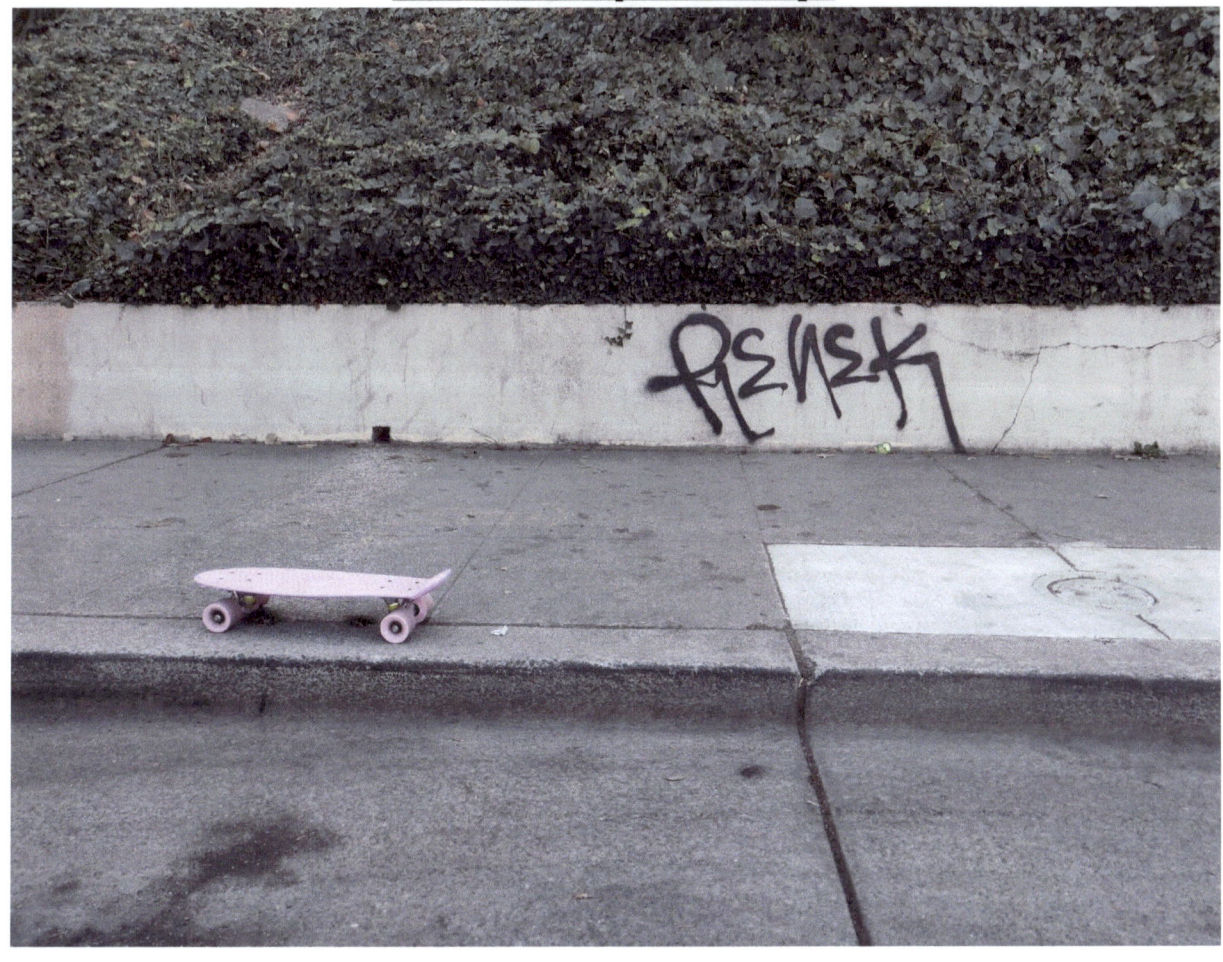

Again we see
in quick hand
a trace of
that storied traveler
of our city,
"Renek"
this time displayed
for all appreciation
in flat black.

<u>Buffing, the Vampire Slayer</u>

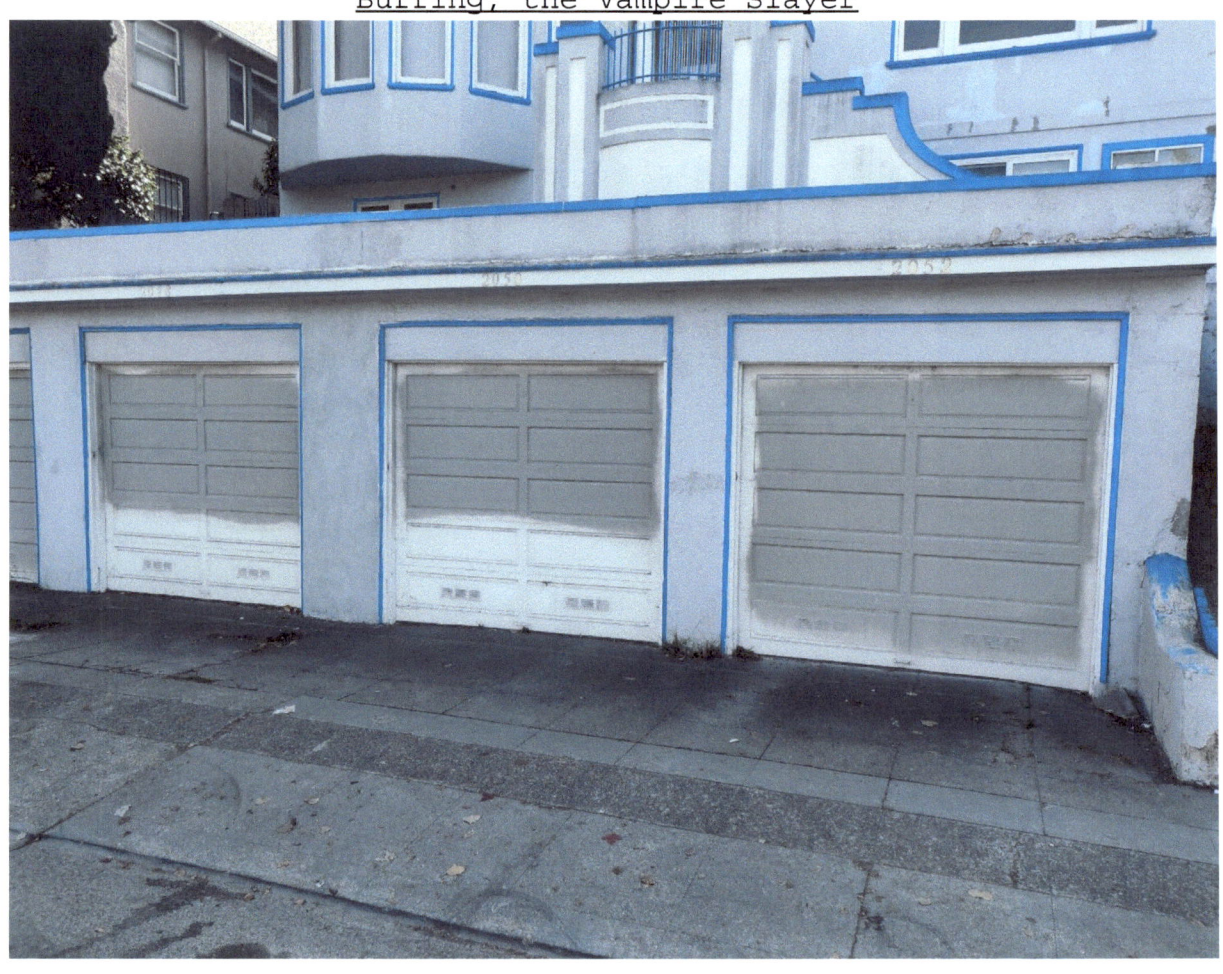

As has been said,
one day you'll look for me
and I'll be gone.
Before where there was
the grace of language,
the subtle artistry
of symbol and form,
are now four patches
of a drab grey,
on a gray building,
with blue accents.

<u>Statement</u>

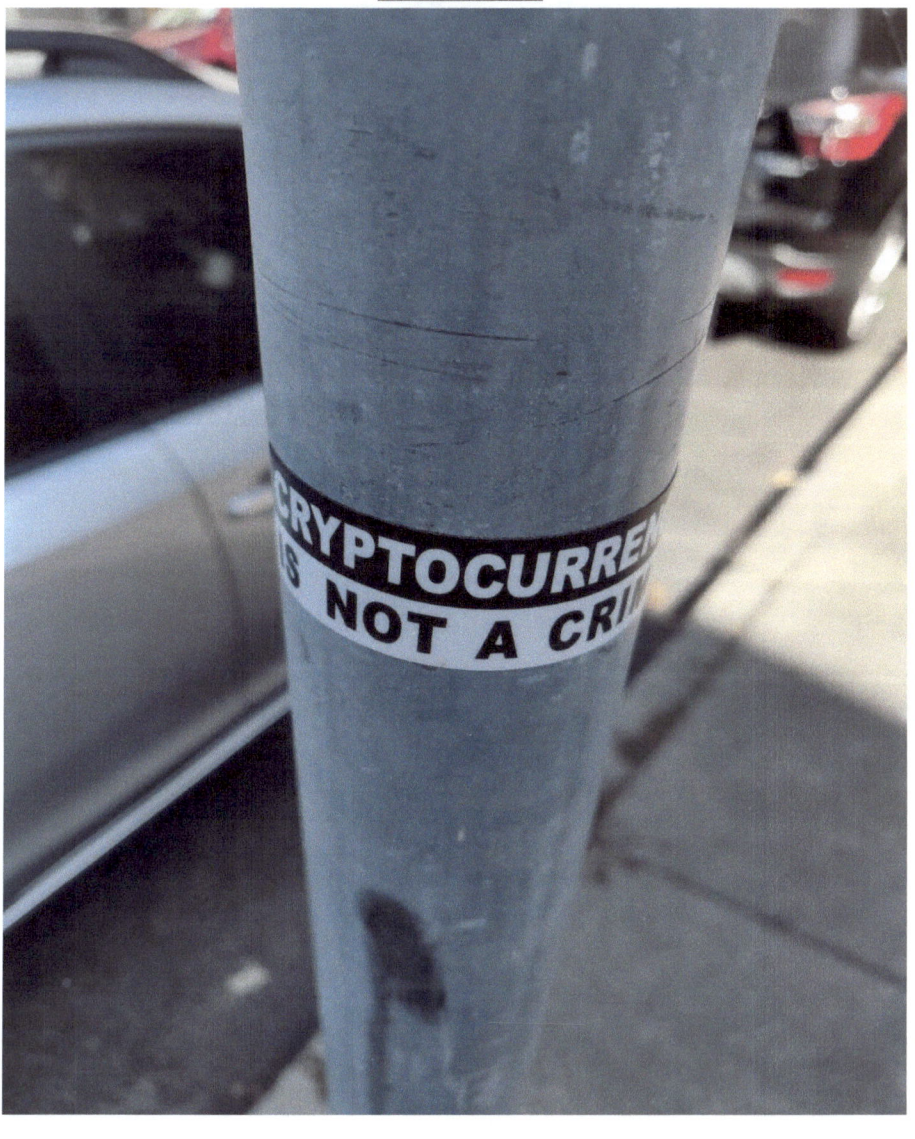

On a small, flat, vinyl
rectangle,
someone left a message.
The rectangle has two
backgrounds, the top
black, and bottom white.
The text on the black is white
and reads:
"CRYPTOCURRENCY"
the text on the white is black
and reads, in continuation
of the above:
"IS NOT A CRIME".

<u>Confusion</u>

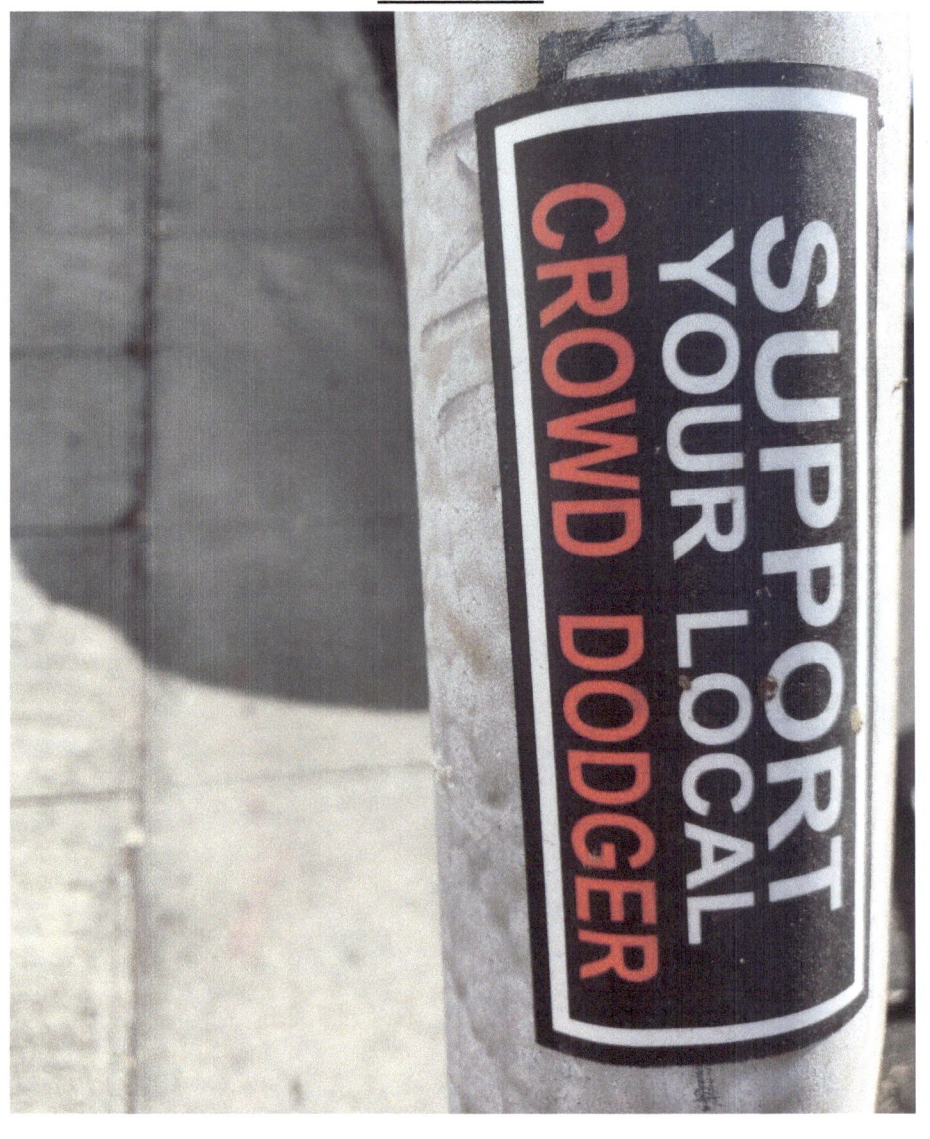

On a sticker-
rectangle type,
Black, with a
white line border
white text-
first-
"support
your local
crowd dodger."
(That last one,
in red.)
What?

<u>Memories</u>

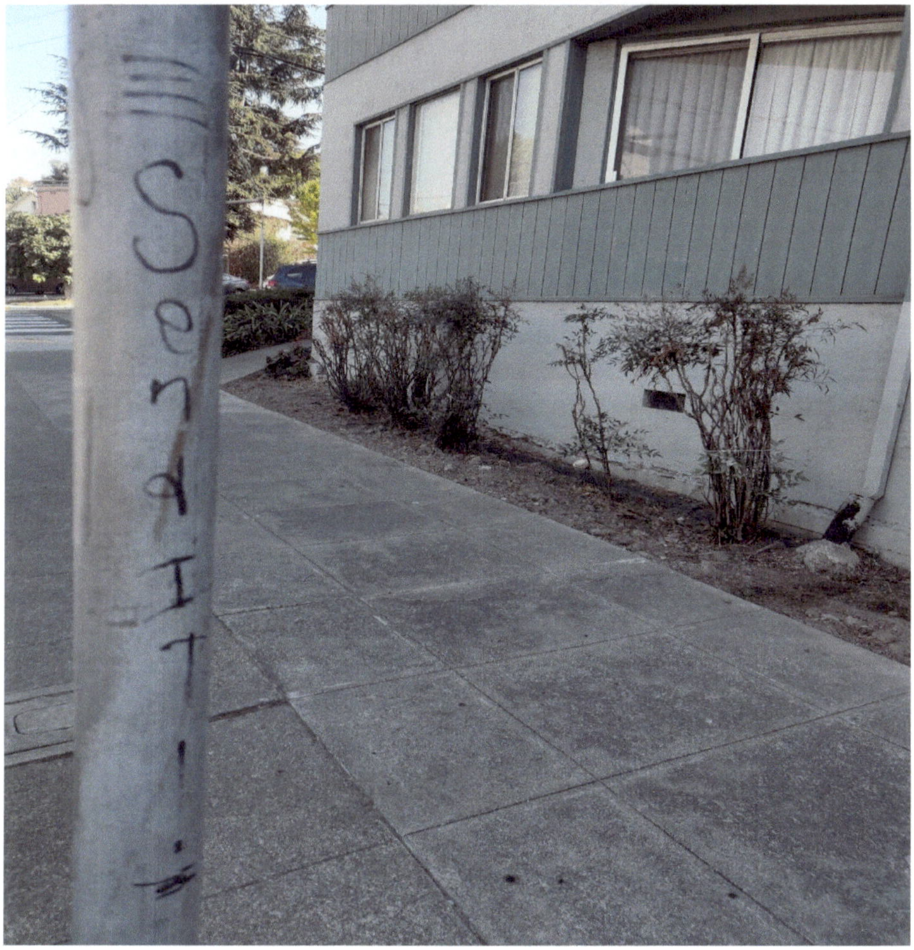

On a pole
(silver)
4 lines
in black Sharpie™
horizontal,
short,
then...
S
E
N
D
I
T
!
Then, another
horizontal line.

<u>Familiar</u>

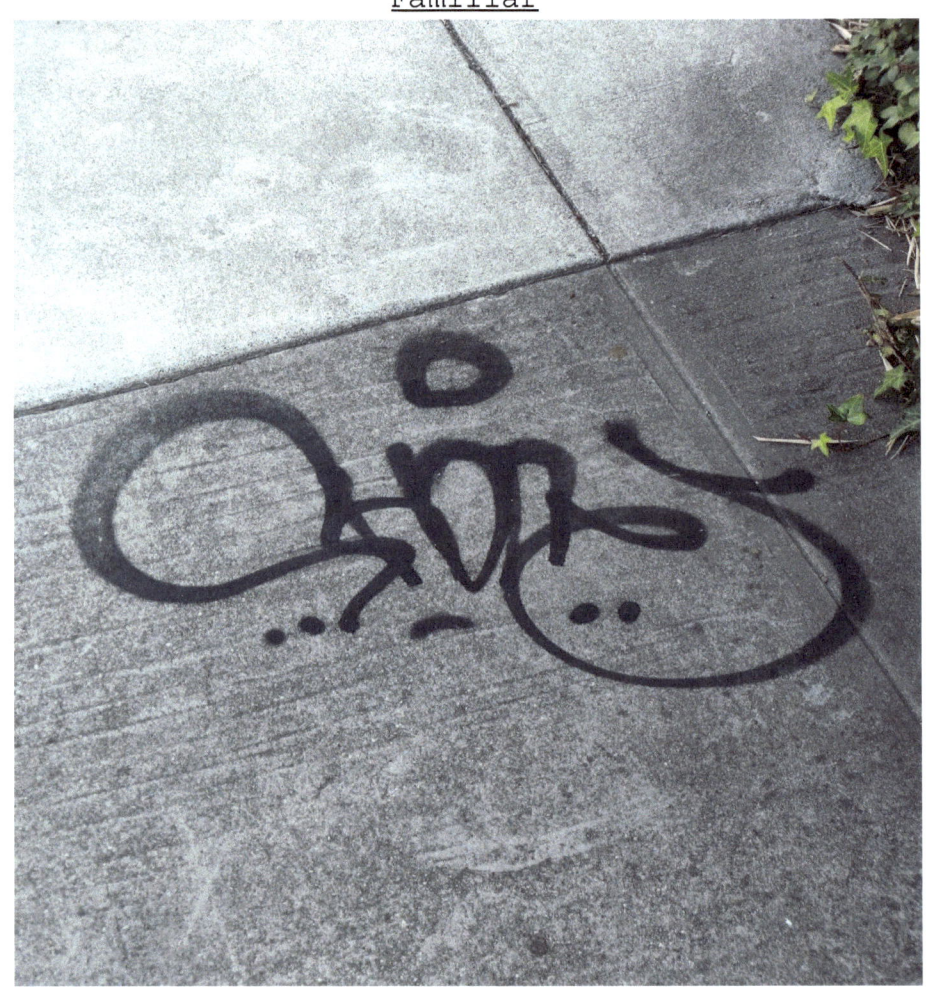

You
are
close at hand.
I see you
every day.
Your deep curves,
by them, i know
you were written
uphill,
My, I can't read you,
what writing.

<u>Trashcan</u>

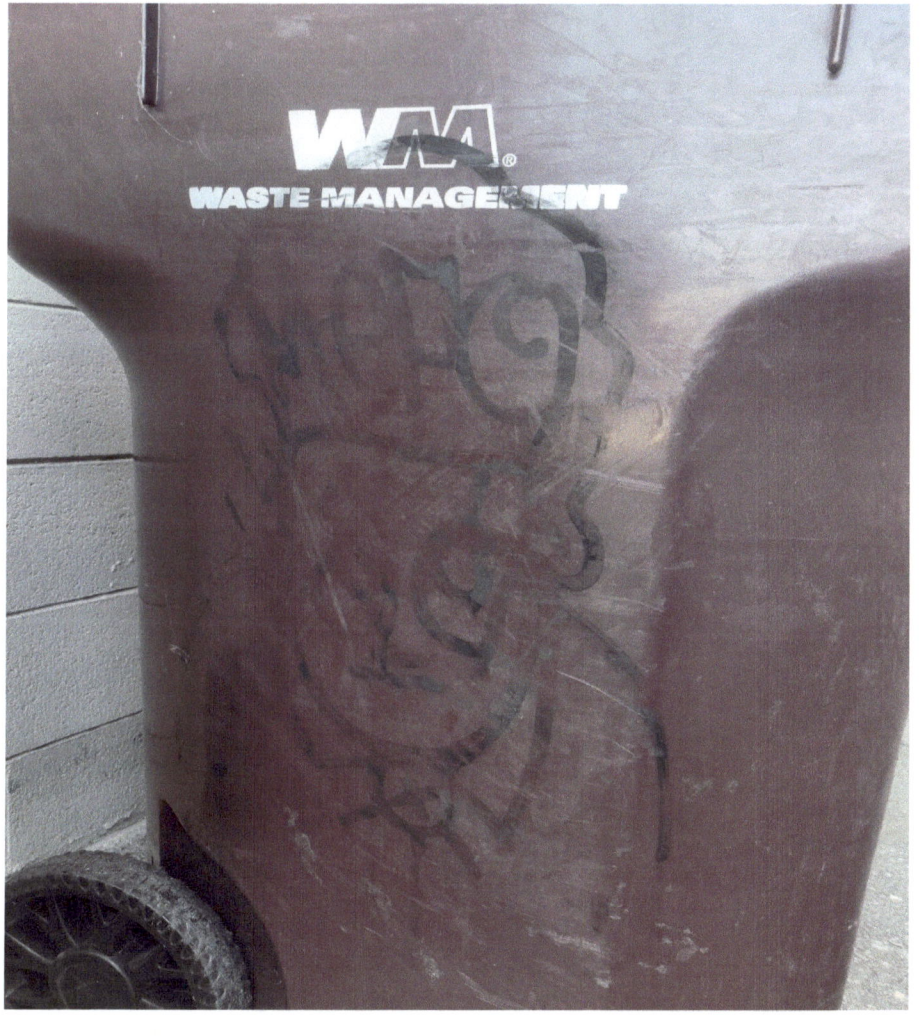

You are familiar
as well,
neighbour, vecino.
On our brown trashcan
in black, thick
marker,
is now a soulful face.
He looks
ashamed,
sad.
In his afro
are the words
"Mepo"
his suit and tie
are crisp.

<u>Green</u>

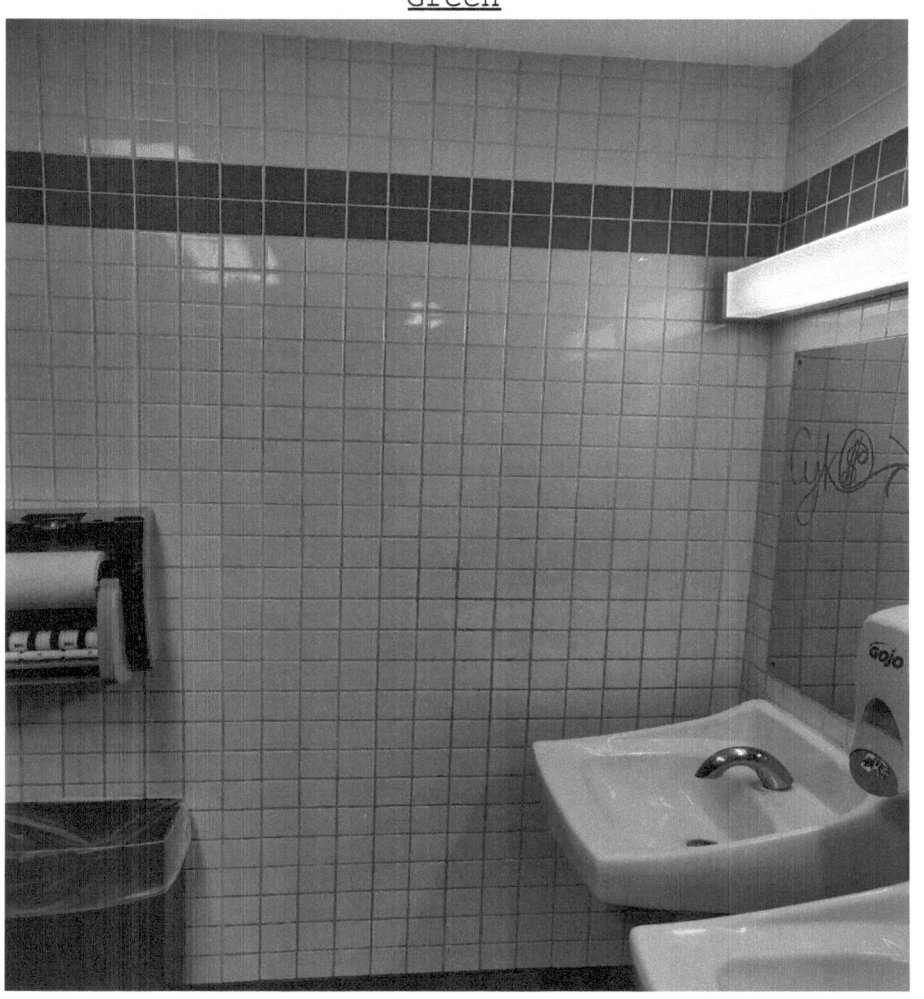

A bathroom
at Laney college
has,
on the left mirror
text of mint green
saying
"Cyko"
with a $
in the "O"
interestingly placed.
The reflection
looks neat.

<u>Sign</u>

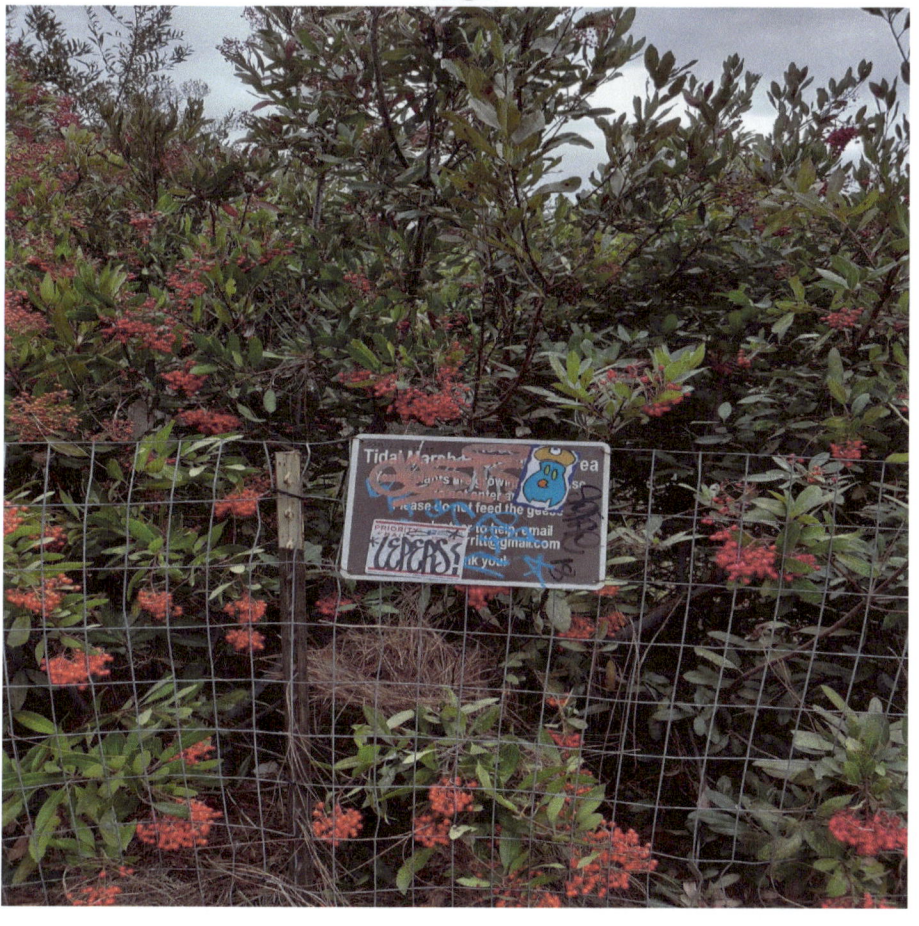

This sign
was meant to explain
about the
tidal marsh area.
But, now, there
are red scrawls,
illegible,
as well as blue.
Two stickers,
one with "Lepers"
2 stars, and a halo
above the middle "E".
The other a blue
bordered postage sticker
a blue face
with green eyes
orange horns.

<u>POSITIVE</u>

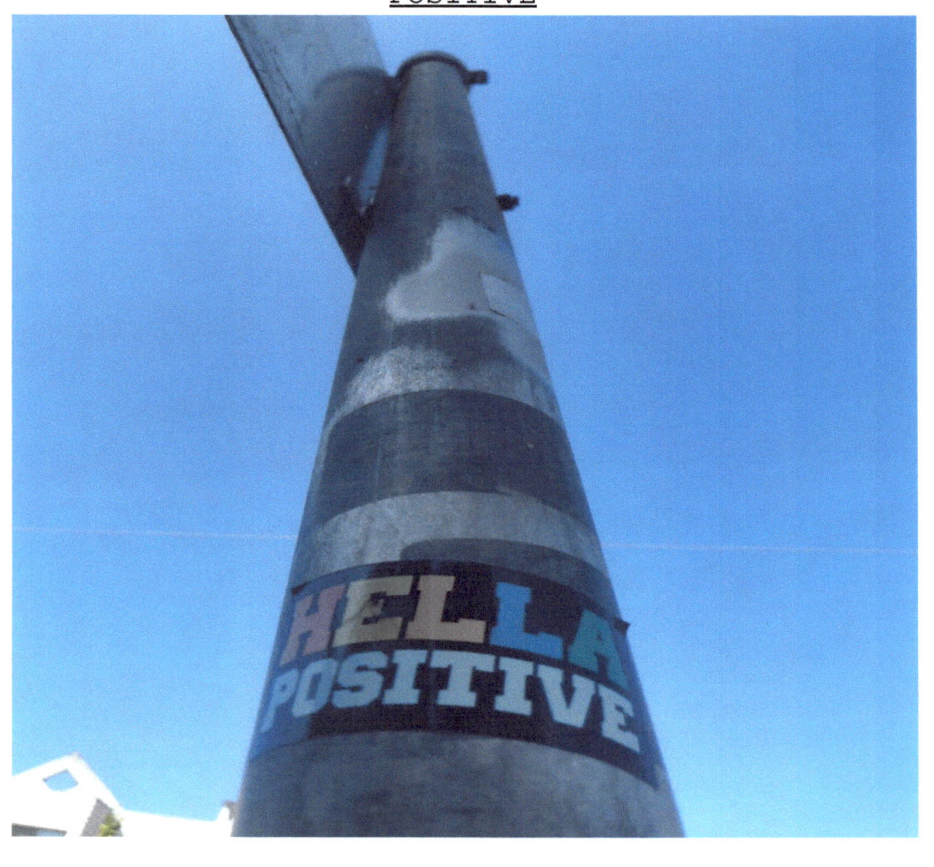

A black sticker
with rainbow letters
saying
"HELLA"
then
in blue,
"POSITIVE."
What a great slogan.

<u>Box</u>

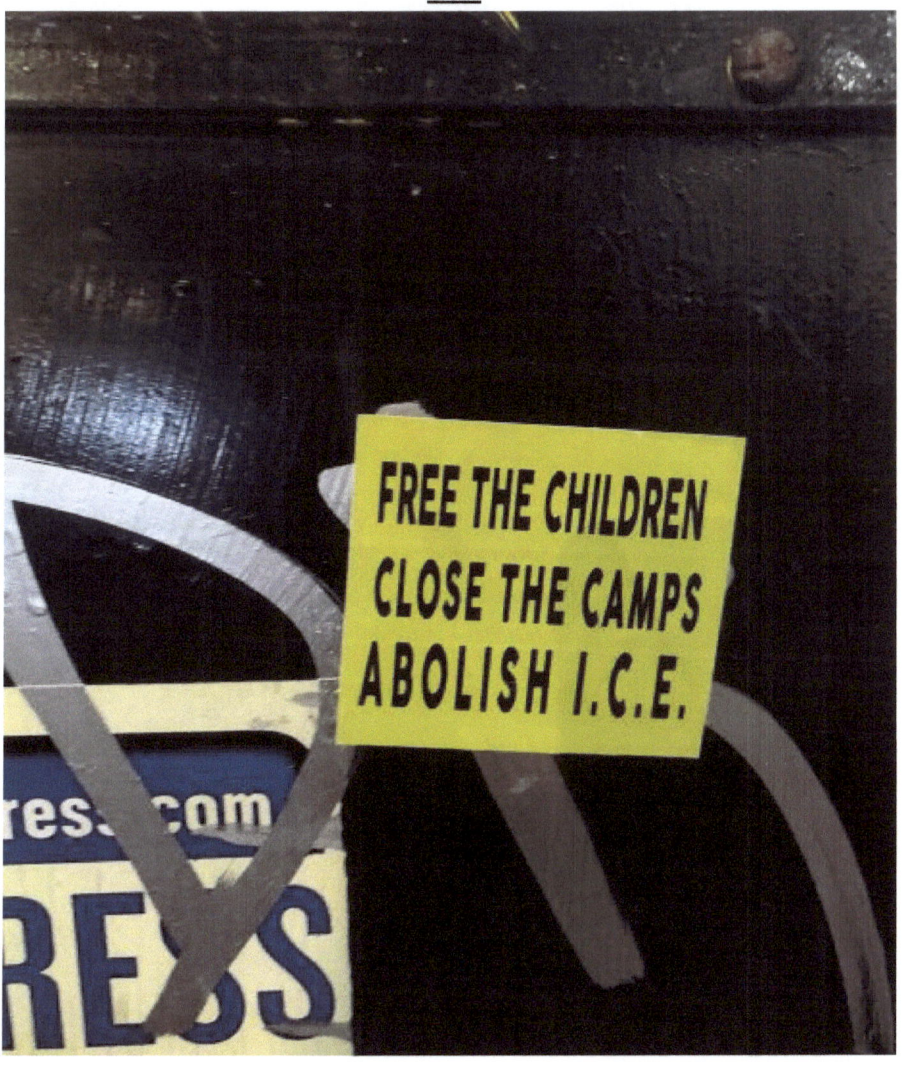

A yellow box
contains black text
3 lines
"FREE THE CHILDREN
CLOSE THE CAMPS
ABOLISH I.C.E."
Says more in
8 words than
many in
a lifetime.

<u>EnLuV</u>

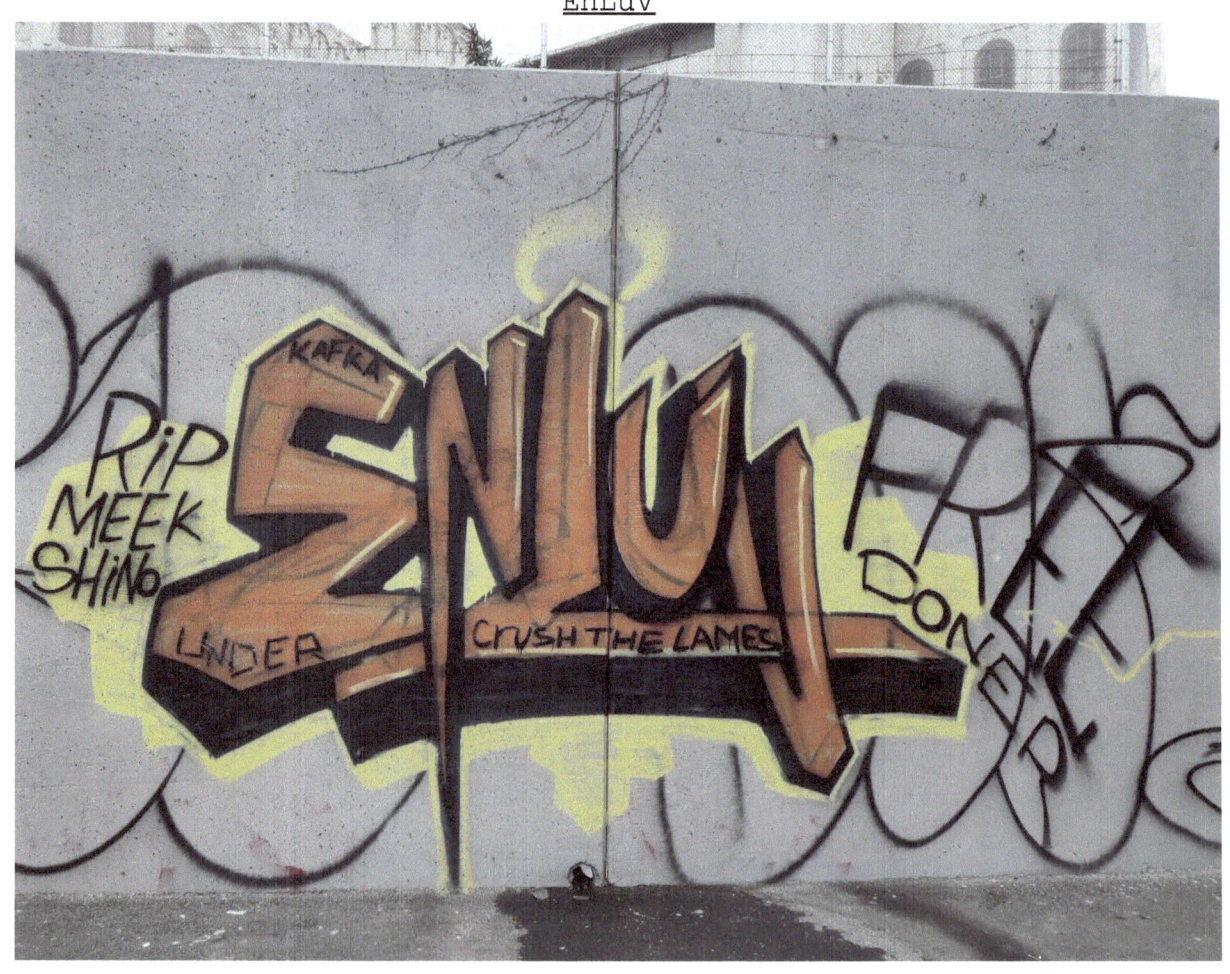

```
Orange stylized block letters
outlined in black
on a concrete wall.
"EnLuv"
but the other text
off sides, in black,
reads more interestingly.
"RiP MEEK SHiNo"
"CRUSH THE LAMES"
"FREE
DONER"
```

<u>Countless</u>

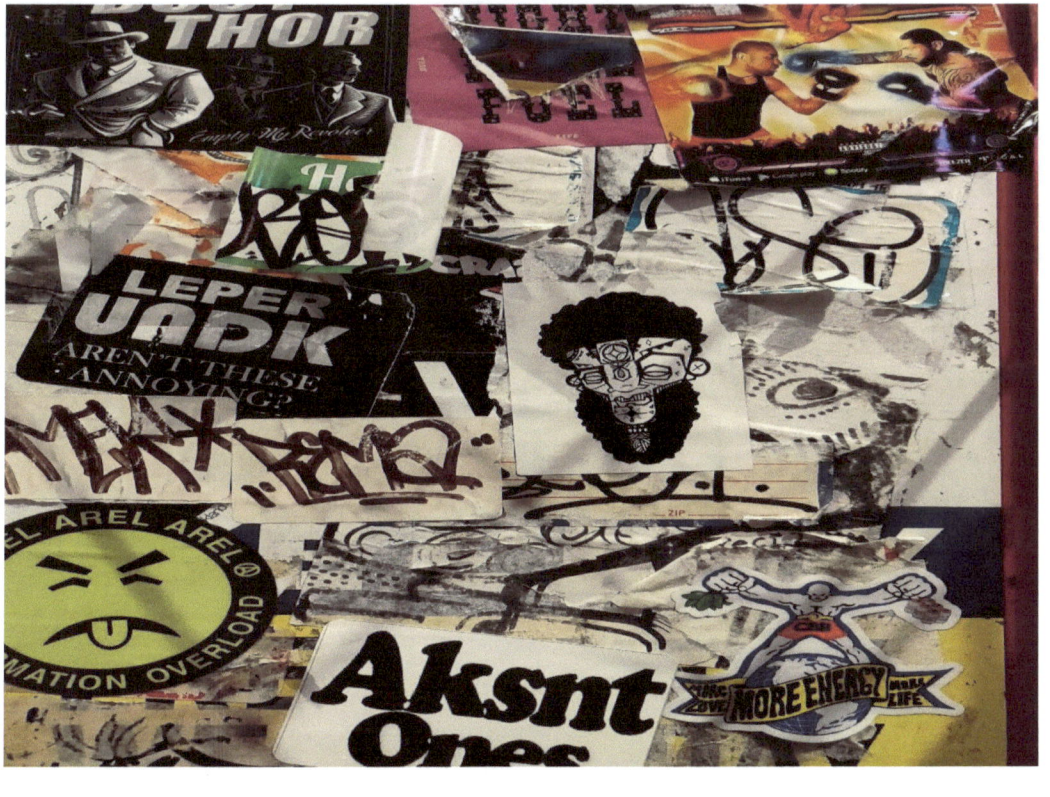

1, 2, 3, 4…
who can say how many
there really are.
Boxing poster
boxing poster
tag sticker
tag sticker
a bejeweled african face
"LEPER UADK
AREN'T THESE ANNOYING?"
in silver on black.
A yellow sick face
with text that doesn't
make sense.
"Aksnt
Ones" (BLK on WHT)
"More energy
more love
more life"
with an atlas
standing on the globe.

The 8

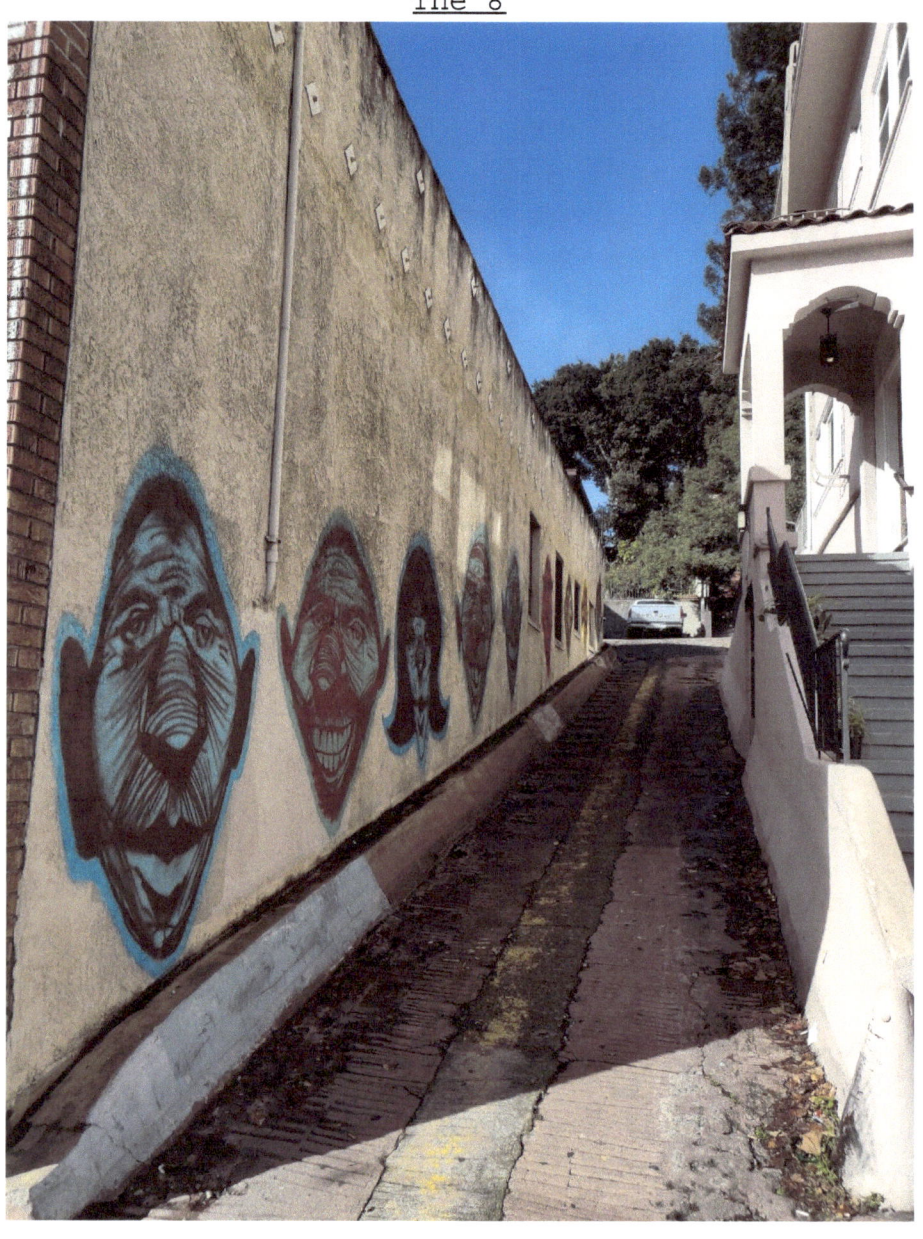

A slew of fucked up faces
like American Horror Story
characters, all,
line a tan wall.
Red and blue, black
and blue, 8 I can
see in view.
Their lips smile
and sneer
as along the wall
they veer.

<u>Fox</u>

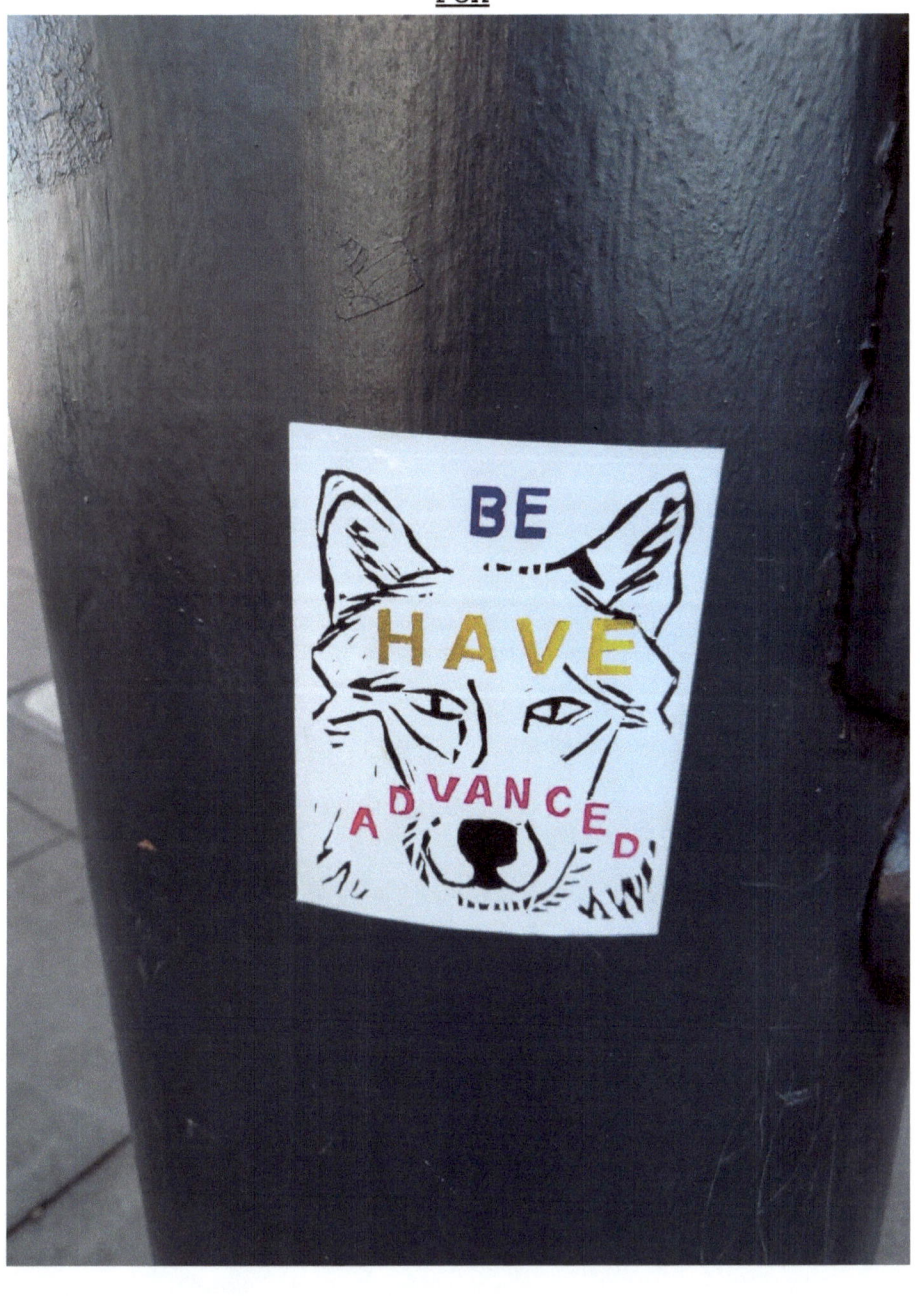

Image of fox, line drawing, black ink
Above: "BE"
Center: "HAVE"
Bottom: "ADVANCED".

Here's a QR code link to my poetry blog!
Any comments are always encouraged.

All designs of graffiti in original mediums represented in this book are owned by their original artists.

All images and poems in this book are property of Grant Schrader © 2020 Schrader

The Photographer and poet does not participate in illegal art activities.